EVOLUTION

Collins

People have always looked at the animals and plants around them and wondered where they came from. Why are there so many different sorts? Do we really need five million different types of beetle? Wouldn't three or four do? What is the point of wasps?

A man called Rudyard Kipling, who was born in 1865, wrote stories such as *How the Camel Got His Hump* and *How the Leopard Got His Spots* to answer this sort of question. For instance, he wrote that the elephant got its nose stretched into a trunk when it was bitten by a crocodile! But those stories were just made up. What really happened?

Kipling might have been
making stories up for fun,
but a man called
Jean-Baptiste Lamarck,
who was born in
1744, thought that
animals and plants
really could be
changed by things
that happened to
them, then pass
those changes on to
the next generation.

Jean-Baptiste Lamarck

So a giraffe, for
instance, by stretching
to reach higher branches,
would grow a slightly longer
neck and this would be passed
on to its **offspring**.

This turned out not to be true, but it got people thinking –
was it possible for animals and plants to change
over time? And if they changed enough, would they turn
into a completely different **species** altogether?

early 19th-century painting of giraffes

Another puzzle was the fact that bones of strange creatures could sometimes be found in the rocks and soil. These fossil skeletons were clearly from animals that no longer existed on Earth. So what had happened to them?

fossil skeleton of a giant ground sloth

EXTINCT MAMMAL

A man called Georges Cuvier, who was born in 1769, worked out two things: firstly, that because the bones of these creatures were found in different layers of rock, they hadn't all become **extinct** at the same time. Species had been coming and going for millions of years. Secondly, that many species of animal,

Georges Cuvier

although they have very different body shapes, share the same pattern of bones. For example, a bat's wing, a whale's flipper and a lion's paw all have the same number and arrangement of bones. This suggested to Cuvier that they perhaps shared an **ancestor**.

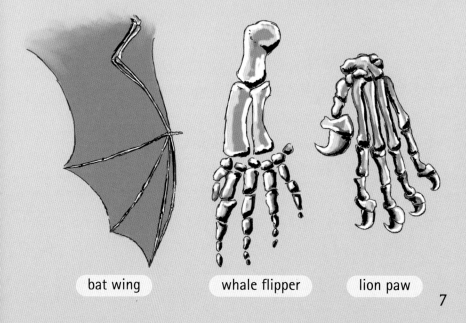

bat wing   whale flipper   lion paw

CHARLES DARWIN AND THE THEORY OF EVOLUTION

Charles Darwin, who was born in 1809 and later went to the University of Cambridge, became interested in natural history, particularly the popular hobby of collecting beetles. After finishing his studies, he went on a number of **geology** field courses, drawing maps of where rocks and fossils could be found in Wales.

Charles Darwin

Darwin was so keen on the natural world that a friend suggested he would be a good person to have along on a trip to map the little-known coast of South America. Someone was needed to map the rocks and collect samples of new plants and animals. The captain of the HMS *Beagle*, Robert FitzRoy, agreed to give Darwin a place on the ship and on 27 December 1831 Darwin set sail.

8

United Kingdom

Atlantic
Ocean

Pacific Ocean

South America

Indian
Ocean

HMS *Beagle*

9

mockingbird

extinct mammal

The voyage of the *Beagle* lasted nearly
five years, during which time the crew drew maps of
the coast and Darwin studied the rocks, collected
specimens of plants and animals and did a lot of thinking.
He found seashells high up in the Andes mountains,
miles from the sea. In the Galapagos Islands he found
mockingbirds, each species slightly different and unique
to its own island.

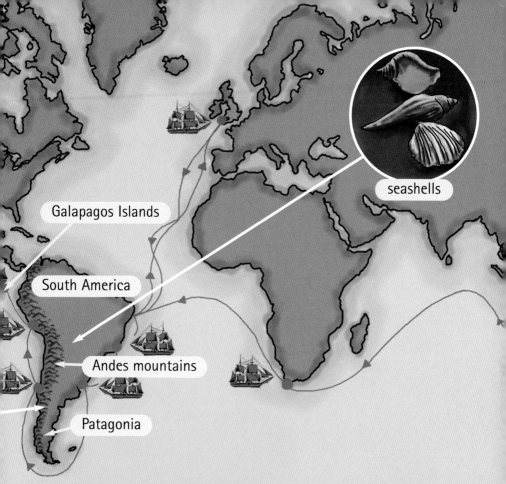

Galapagos Islands

South America

Andes mountains

Patagonia

seashells

In Patagonia he found the bones of huge extinct mammals alongside modern species. It seemed as though the Earth had shifted and changed over millions of years and that some species had died out, while new ones had appeared.

All these strange discoveries were carefully recorded in Darwin's **journal** and some of his findings were sent on ahead to London. So by the time the HMS *Beagle* docked in Cornwall on 2 October 1836, Darwin was already a celebrity.

Darwin had a problem, though. All his thinking on that five-year voyage had convinced him that it was possible for one species, over time, to change into another. But before publishing his ideas Darwin needed lots of evidence.

Charles Darwin studying

So he studied hard. He wanted to not only show that "evolution", as it was now being called, could happen, but also how it happened. He had an idea that individuals that were best suited to their surroundings – the "fittest" individuals – would survive to mate and pass on that advantage to the next generation. The ones that were less fit would die before they could mate. This was called "survival of the fittest", or "natural selection".

The largest bird reaches the prey first, leading over time to "survival of the fittest".

Darwin spent many years studying things like pigeon breeding and the lives of earthworms, looking at evidence to back up his theory of evolution. It was clear, for instance, that humans could change animals and plants by choosing which ones got to **breed**.

Farmers have always done this. If they want big, strong cattle, they breed the biggest and strongest bulls; if they want excellent wool they breed the sheep with the best wool. Over time, the animals change and improve – most farm animals and crops are now very, very different to their wild ancestors. Nature makes the same choices, Darwin believed, about which animals get to breed.

Of course, nature doesn't really "choose". Some animals are born with **characteristics** that give them a better chance of surviving, like a cheetah that can run just a little bit faster than all the other cheetahs. A faster cheetah will be able to catch more food. More food will mean the cheetah will be stronger, healthier and more likely to attract a mate. Slower cheetahs will go hungry, be less healthy and might even die before they have a chance to breed.

And so these characteristics – like being able to run faster – are passed on from parents to offspring. Just like the farmers had done, nature favours the best characteristics and slowly the species changes into something new.

So people began to believe that animals and plants could change over time and that there had been many thousands of creatures that had died out in the past, leaving only their fossil bones behind.

Finally, in 1859, Darwin felt he had enough evidence and published his book *On the Origin of Species*. In it, he set out his ideas about how species gradually changed over time and supported it all with examples from his studies.

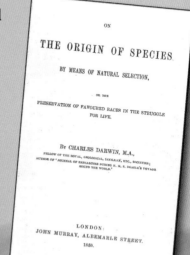

ON

THE ORIGIN OF SPECIES

BY MEANS OF NATURAL SELECTION,

OR THE

PRESERVATION OF FAVOURED RACES IN THE STRUGGLE FOR LIFE.

By CHARLES DARWIN, M.A.,

FELLOW OF THE ROYAL, GEOLOGICAL, LINNEAN, ETC., SOCIETIES; AUTHOR OF ' JOURNAL OF RESEARCHES DURING H. M. S. BEAGLE'S VOYAGE ROUND THE WORLD.'

LONDON:

JOHN MURRAY, ALBEMARLE STREET.

1859.

The right of Translation is reserved.

title page of
On the Origin of Species

So, is the change from one species to another gradual, happening over millions of years, or does it happen more suddenly? Darwin wasn't sure. After all, some animals and plants, like the shark and the Wollemi pine tree, have hardly changed at all over millions of years.

shark from
millions of years ago

modern shark

Wollemi pine tree from millions of years ago

modern Wollemi pine tree

At some points in history, however, there seem to have been explosions of evolution, with thousands of new species appearing in a relatively short time. To find out why, we need to go right back to the origins of life on Earth.

For many millions of years the sea was the safest place to live. The land was swept by violent hurricanes and huge tidal waves and baked by fierce sunlight. During the Cambrian Period, which started 542 million years ago, many creatures that would be familiar today appeared in the oceans, such as tiny snail-like animals with shells and early **crustaceans** – relatives of modern shrimps and lobsters.

One group that was particularly successful in this period was the trilobites. These marine creatures looked like giant woodlice and over 300 million years they evolved into an amazing 17,000 different species. The first trilobites were small and plain, but by the end of their time on Earth they had well-developed eyes and some of them grew strange spines and horns on their shells. The trilobites became one of the biggest groups of animals on Earth.

two species
of trilobite

trilobite

By the Ordovician Period, which began 488 million years ago, the amount of oxygen in Earth's atmosphere meant that it was now safe to live on land. We know from fossil burrows, probably made by creatures similar to millipedes, that there was life on dry land around 450 million years ago. The first land plants and fungi appeared not long after.

trilobites

nautiloid

In the seas, the trilobites were facing competition from two new groups of creatures – fish and nautiloids – and eventually the trilobites died out. Nautiloids are relatives of the modern-day squid and octopus. The earliest ones had long, straight shells. As they evolved to become larger, this long shell became hard to **manoeuvre**. Nautiloids with curved shells began to appear, followed eventually by the spiral-shelled ammonites.

ammonites

By the start of the Carboniferous Period, which began 363 million years ago, many creatures that would be familiar to us lived both on land and in the sea. Sharks roamed the oceans and a wide range of insects lived on land among the ferns and pine trees. In shallow waters, a group of fish called tetrapods ("four feet") were evolving the tools needed to move out on to dry land.

This may have been the best way to escape predators like sharks, plus there was food to be found on land that nothing else was eating.

tetrapod

shark

The earliest tetrapods were very fish-like and probably used stiff fins to move through mud from one pool to another. This would stop them getting trapped if the pool dried out.

very early tetrapod:
Eusthenopteron

Later tetrapods such as *Ichthyostega* looked much more like modern-day amphibians, such as newts and salamanders, but were still only capable of spending short periods out of water.

Ichthyostega

By 295 million years ago, these tetrapods had evolved into creatures such as *Eryops*, which breathed air using lungs and had a stiff backbone to stop it sagging without the support of water.

Eryops

THE RULE OF THE DINOSAURS

Over 240 million years, those primitive tetrapods that crawled on to land had transformed into both the dinosaurs and the very earliest mammals. Predators such as *Allosaurus* stalked giant **sauropods** like *Camarasaurus*. Flying reptiles such as *Pterodactylus* and *Rhamphorhynchus* roamed the skies, while on the ground a small dinosaur with feathers, *Archaeopteryx*, was to become the ancestor of today's birds.

Rhamphorhynchus

Archaeopteryx

This explosion of new species was caused by changes taking place in the world. The continents of Earth were not fixed in place; they moved around the planet very slowly in a process called the "continental drift". As they did, they carried animals and plants to new places. So creatures from the tropics might have ended up near the South Pole and needed to change and adapt. As the plants changed, animals evolved to eat them, and as those plant-eaters changed, new predators evolved to eat them, and so on.

Pterodactylus

Camarasaurus

Allosaurus

As a huge landmass called Pangaea split up and gradually drifted apart to form the modern continents, the dinosaurs found themselves in a wide range of different habitats, from cool northern forests to hot deserts. These changes forced them to adapt and, as they did, they became bigger – and stranger!

Pangaea 250 million years ago

PANGAEA

the continents breaking up during the Jurassic Period

the continents today

NORTH AMERICA

ASIA

AFRICA

SOUTH AMERICA

AUSTRALIA

ANTARCTICA

Protoceratops was a typical four-legged dinosaur. It didn't look much different to hundreds of other dinosaurs that had gone before it, except for two things: it had a beaked mouth, a bit like a parrot, and a frill on the back of its skull. Nobody really knows what the frill was for, but *Protoceratops* lived in the same part of the world as the predator *Velociraptor*, so perhaps it was to protect its neck from bites.

Whatever the reason, from then on all of *Protoceratops'* relatives had beaked mouths and different variations of the neck shield. Many of them also had horns.

Velociraptor

Protoceratops

Triceratops had three horns and a bony shield. *Einiosaurus* had a nose-horn that curved forward. *Pentaceratops* had an enormous shield over its neck. *Styracosaurus* had a frill edged with huge spikes and *Pachyrhinosaurus* was probably the craziest of all – spikes, horns, lumps and bumps! Nobody really knows why there were so many variations – as with *Protoceratops*, the horns and spikes were probably for defence against giant meat-eaters like *Tyrannosaurus*. But the shields could have been for protection, losing heat or even signalling to a mate in the breeding season.

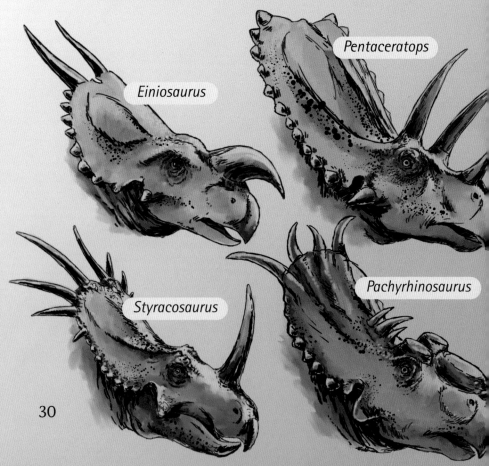

Pentaceratops

Einiosaurus

Styracosaurus

Pachyrhinosaurus

Tyrannosaurus

Triceratops

31

So, it's clear that times of change spark bursts of rapid evolution. And at the end of the Cretaceous Period, about 65 million years ago, came one of the biggest changes of all. Around half of all animal species, including all the dinosaurs, disappeared. It's now generally agreed that a massive meteor hit the Earth off the coast of Mexico, throwing millions of tonnes of gas and dust into the atmosphere.

The oceans were less badly affected, but on land the few remaining groups of animals that survived were suddenly free to adapt and fill all the empty spaces. One particular group, who had been waiting quietly in the shadow of the dinosaurs, were the mammals.

MAMMALS AND BIRDS TAKE OVER

The first mammals appeared 215 million years ago, at around the time of the first dinosaurs. But while the dinosaurs had evolved into a huge range of shapes and sizes, the mammals had remained small and mouse-like. However, with the dinosaurs out of the way and so much food available, mammals were free to become bigger and more specialised.

Paraceratherium

Andrewsarchus

Paraceratherium, an ancestor of the modern-day rhino, was probably the largest land animal that ever lived. It stood around five and a half metres at the shoulder and with its head raised reached as high as eight metres. The mammoths, closely related to today's elephants, were nearly as big. Such large **herbivores** resulted in the evolution of predators big enough to hunt them. One of the biggest was *Andrewsarchus*, known only from a single fossil skull 83 centimetres long.

mammoth

But what about the birds?

For many years, people thought that all dinosaurs were scaly, like modern-day crocodiles. In fact, scraps of fossil skin had been found that seemed to back this up.
But then a discovery was made that changed all that – fuzzy dinosaurs!

Sinosauropteryx was a small dinosaur found in China. Its fossils were the first to show the remains of a fuzzy down of very simple feathers. These were thin, hollow tubes, very different to modern bird feathers. They wouldn't have been used for flying. In fact, *Sinosauropteryx* had arms instead of wings. So clearly its feathers were for something else, perhaps to keep it warm or attract a mate. Whatever their original use, over time they became more like real feathers. It's likely that they would have helped the very small dinosaurs to glide, possibly to escape predators or to catch insects.

fossil of a *Sinosauropteryx*

Sinosauropteryx

By 1861, just two years after Darwin's *On the Origin of Species* was published, the first real bird-like fossil had been discovered – *Archaeopteryx*. It was a small dinosaur with proper feathers and well-developed wings that could clearly fly. It lived in the Late Jurassic, when dinosaurs ruled the Earth. So *Archaeopteryx* seems to be a halfway stage between a reptile and a bird. Then, gradually over time, the relatives of *Archaeopteryx* grew bigger arms and stronger chest muscles and gliding turned into true flight – the first birds took to the skies.

Archaeopteryx

So, is evolution still taking place, or is it just something that happened millions of years ago?

Well, natural selection works very, very slowly, but it's still possible to see it in action today.

A good example of modern-day evolution is the peppered moth. The factory chimneys of the **Industrial Revolution** made many tree trunks black with soot. Pale peppered moths were easy to spot against this dark background and were more likely to be eaten by birds. Some moths were born with dark wings and these were more likely to survive and pass on this new colour, so dark moths became common. Now that air quality is better and trees are generally much cleaner, the pale moths are once again the most common.

THE FUTURE OF EVOLUTION

If evolution is still taking place, where might it go in the future? A group of scientists have tried to predict what the world would look like in five million, 100 million and 200 million years. They predict a world where seven-tonne squid walk on land, snails hop like kangaroos and fish fly through forests like birds.

Of course, this is all guesswork and it's impossible to know what will happen in the far distant future. But one thing is sure; whatever changes take place, Darwin's big idea – natural selection – will provide a way for life to adapt.

GLOSSARY

ancestor   an early species of animal that others have evolved from

breed   to have babies

characteristics   typical qualities belonging to a species

crustaceans   types of creatures with four or more pairs of limbs, including crabs, lobsters and woodlice

extinct   a type of animal or plant that no longer exists

geology   the study of what the Earth is made of

herbivores   animals that eat only plants

Industrial Revolution   when the invention of steam-powered machines in the 1800s led to the creation of large towns with many factories

journal   a book in which a daily record of events is written

manoeuvre   a movement that needs some skill to carry out

offspring   an animal's young

sauropods   very large herbivore dinosaurs with long necks and small heads, such as the *Diplodocus*

species   individuals that can breed together

INDEX

EVOLUTION TIMELINE

Cambrian
Period

Ordovician
Period

Carboniferous
Period

Cretaceous Period | Jurassic Period | meteor hits Earth | mammals

:: Ideas for reading ::

Written by Linda Pagett B.Ed(hons), M.Ed
Lecturer and Educational Consultant

Learning objectives: identify and summarise information from a text; use knowledge of different organisational features of texts to find information effectively; interrogate texts to deepen and clarify understanding and response; offer reasons and evidence for their views, considering alternative opinions

Curriculum links: Science: Interdependence and adaptation

Interest words: ammonites, ancestor, breed, Carboniferous, characteristics, Cretaceous, crustaceans, extinct, geology, herbivore, Industrial Revolution, journal, jurassic, manoeuvre, nautiloids, offspring, Ordovician, Pangaea, Patagonia, sauropods, species, tetrapods

Resources: whiteboard, collage materials, globe

Getting started

This book can be read over two or more guided reading sessions.

- Ask children if they have heard the word *evolution*. Read the blurb, and as a group discuss whether they could answer the question and what children think evolution might be.

- Look at the cover together and discuss the artwork. Do they see similarities between the three creatures? Can they think of any reasons for this?

- Turn to the glossary and make sure children are confident with using it, and understand the definitions.

Reading and responding

- Read pp2-3 together and ask children how they think elephants got their trunks, and to give ideas for how other animals developed into their current form, e.g. why a tiger has stripes. Write these ideas on the whiteboard to return to later.

- Ask children to read to the end of p7 in pairs. Discuss the word *ancestor* and check their understanding of the term. What animal could this have been and what would it have looked like?